Wetlands

By Anastasia Suen

CELEBRATION PRESS
Pearson Learning Group

Contents

Welcome to the Wetlands

A flock of mallard ducks spots a patch of water and flies down to rest and eat. The place where they land is called a prairie pothole. Most ducks in North America are born in prairie potholes like this one.

Prairie potholes were formed long ago. Glacier ice scraped these holes in the ground. The low spots still collect water and stay wet for much of the year. The tall grass that grows around the potholes hides the mallards from **predators**. The ducks can safely eat plant seeds there.

In North America, 50 to 80 percent of the ducks raise their young in prairie potholes.

Prairie potholes, found across the northern Great Plains, are a kind of marsh. Along with bogs, fens, and swamps, marshes are one of four major types of wetlands. All four types are found in the United States. A wetland is simply land that is wet. Some wetlands have water in them every day, while others have wet and dry seasons.

An area needs to be wet for only part of the year to be called a wetland. Scientists look at how long the growing season is for an area. If the ground is wet for at least 7.5 percent of the growing season, then that area is a wetland even if the ground is dry for the rest of the time.

There are different kinds of wetlands. The type of water found in a wetland is one way to tell it from other kinds. Wetland areas found inland are almost always freshwater wetlands. In fact, 95 percent of our wetlands have fresh water. Coastal wetlands, in contrast, often have salty water. They may lie at the ocean's edge in places where rivers meet the sea. The plants that grow in wetlands are another way to tell them apart. Grasses are found in marshes and fens. Shrubs and trees grow in swamps. Bogs produce moss.

Swamps, Marshes, Bogs, and Fens

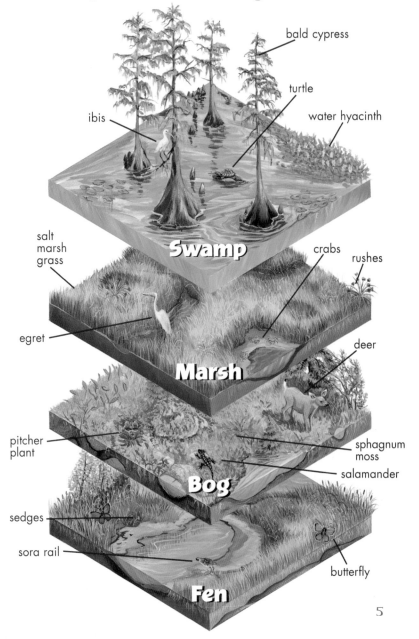

bald cypress

turtle

water hyacinth

ibis

Swamp

salt marsh grass

crabs

rushes

egret

Marsh

deer

pitcher plant

sphagnum moss

salamander

Bog

sedges

sora rail

butterfly

Fen

Swamps

Two different-colored Northern Water Snakes
in a Louisiana cypress swamp

It's hard to imagine that alligators live just miles
from the stadium in New Orleans where the
Super Bowl is sometimes played! Outside the city,
catfish, crayfish, and frogs, along with alligators,
swim in swamps. Poisonous cottonmouth snakes
slither under cypress and gum trees. Birds such as
herons, hawks, egrets, eagles, and ibis feed in the
water and nest in the trees. Deer, raccoons,
beavers, wild boar, and black bears call swamps
home, too.

A swamp is a wetland dominated by woody plants that has water on the ground for at least part of the year. Swamps near rivers often act as **floodplains** when heavy rains cause a river to flow over its banks. If you visit a river swamp during the rainy season, it looks as if the river flows right through the forest.

Not all trees can grow in standing water. Some die when their roots are wet for long periods of time. Plants that are able to live in either water or very wet soil are called **hydrophytes**.

Cypress trees are hydrophytes. The base of these trees is wide, helping them to stand in the water. Woody knobs poke above the water to help the roots take in oxygen.

Mangrove trees grow in swamps found along the coast. These trees are able to survive in both salt and fresh water. Mangroves have multiple roots that can be seen above the water. The tree looks as if it has branches reaching both up and down! However, you can easily tell the branches from the roots because the roots don't have leaves on them. Mangrove swamps are home to many kinds of birds, ranging from pelicans to flamingos.

Spanish moss is not a true moss. It is closely related to the pineapple tree.

Another plant that thrives in a swamp is Spanish moss. The Spanish moss that hangs from the trees in swampy areas uses the trees for support. It has no roots in the ground. It absorbs food and water from the damp swamp air, making it an **epiphyte**.

Skunk cabbage also grows well in the swamp. As the first plant to come up out of the snow in the spring, it produces heat that melts the snow. This plant was named for the skunklike smell it gives off.

The American alligator has 80 teeth.

The wild places in the swamp are home to many creatures. American alligators live in swamps in the South. Perfectly adapted for swamp living, the alligator's eyes and nose are on top of its head, allowing it to stay submerged in the water for long periods of time. Looking like a floating log, it blends in with the swamp as it waits for its next meal. When prey comes near, the alligator lunges and grabs it. Alligators eat fish, frogs, turtles, birds, small mammals, and even smaller alligators.

We think of bears as roaming through woodlands, yet they can be found in the Okefenokee Swamp in Georgia. The black bear is **omnivorous**, eating both plants and meat. It eats berries, nuts, and roots, as well as insects, fish, eggs, and smaller animals. Black bears also use their sharp claws to dig up turtle nests to find tasty eggs.

Among the different kinds of turtles found in swamps are painted turtles, which are brightly marked. Young painted turtles are **carnivorous**. They eat meat, including maggots, larvae, and beetles. As they grow, the turtles become omnivorous, eating plants as well as leeches, snails, tadpoles, crayfish, and smaller fish. As painted turtles grow older still, they become more **herbivorous**. Plants become their main food source.

Many fish make their homes in the ponds and streams of the swamp. Not surprisingly, the big fish eat the small fish, and the small fish eat the tiny fish. Fish also eat the various insects and plants that float in the muddy swamp water.

Marshes

Marshes can be saltwater or freshwater. Saltwater marshes lie near coastlines. They are home to many creatures.

In the saltwater marshes of the Chesapeake Bay, mummichogs, or mud minnows, dart through the shallow water. Blue crabs scurry along the muddy bottom looking for food, and clams and mud shrimps burrow in the mud. Long-legged birds like egrets and ibis step through the grass, and ducks and coots swim by.

The Chesapeake Bay has over 4,000 miles of shoreline.

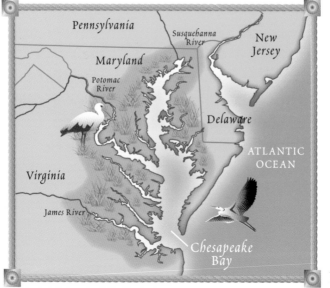

The name "Chesapeake" comes from a Native American word meaning "Great Shellfish Bay." This bay flows along the coast of Virginia and divides Maryland into two parts. It is the largest **estuary** in the United States, with 4,400 miles of shoreline.

All along the shore, about 50 streams and rivers carry fresh water into the bay. Most of this fresh water comes from three main rivers—the Susquehanna, the Potomac, and the James. The water from these rivers mixes with the salty water from the sea as the ocean tides rise and fall.

Some of these **tidal** marshes contain mostly fresh water, though they rise and fall with the tides. They are freshwater tidal marshes. Many of the same creatures that live in a saltwater marsh live here. Herons, egrets, ducks, mummichogs, and blue crabs can be found in both types of marshes.

A freshwater tidal marsh is also home to creatures that cannot live in salt water. Rat snakes and water snakes live in the fresh water. So do painted and snapping turtles. Frogs, toads, and salamanders also make their homes there.

The grasses look different, too. Tall cattails grow in the freshwater tidal marsh. Wild rice and river bulrush also grow there.

Inland freshwater marshes lie far from ocean waters. They are the most common types of marshes in the United States. They can be found from Alaska to Florida, from the Great Plains to mountaintops.

Inland marshes occur in the shallow waters at the edges of ponds, lakes, and rivers. Bulrushes, cattails, and reeds grow in the soggy soil. The water varies from a few inches to three feet deep and sometimes dries out completely.

A muskrat makes its home in the marsh.

The inland marsh provides a home for muskrats, otters, and birds that eat fish. Sometimes muskrats eat crayfish, clams, or frogs, but they are usually herbivorous. These animals feed on the **aquatic** plants that grow in the water of the inland marsh. They eat the roots and stems of cattails, sedges, lilies, and grasses.

The muskrat uses aquatic plants for both food and shelter. It builds its home, called a lodge, in the water. The lodge is built by mixing cattails and other aquatic plants with mud and branches.

Not only is the water the muskrat's home, it also protects the muskrat from predators such as foxes, raccoons, and minks. Raptors, such as herons, hawks, and owls, also feed on muskrats. To escape these predators, the muskrat swims back to its lodge. The only entrance to a muskrat lodge is under the water, so once inside, the muskrat is safe. If the muskrat cannot reach its lodge, it can swim under water to avoid capture. A muskrat can swim under water for 15 minutes without coming up for air.

Types of Inland Marshes

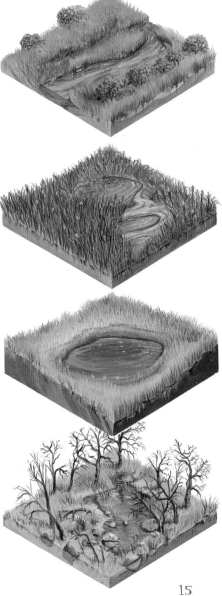

Wet meadows form in poorly drained areas. They rely on rainfall for their water and are often dry in the summer.

Prairie potholes, found in the Upper Midwest, rely on both groundwater and precipitation from rain and snow.

Playa lakes, found in the desertlike regions of the southern High Plains, are formed when heavy spring rainfall fills the shallow desert holes. Most are dry after the water evaporates.

Shallow vernal pools are usually found in gently sloping grasslands. They rely on rainfall for their water. During winter and spring, vernal pools may fill and dry out several times.

🪷 Bogs and Fens

As a fly buzzes around the North Carolina bog, a sweet scent catches its attention. The fly moves closer, touching the hairs on the pretty red leaf. *Snap!* The fly is doomed. The leaf closes over the fly, and the Venus' flytrap begins digesting it. The leaf is sealed shut and won't open for days.

The Venus' flytrap is a carnivorous plant. It produces a special liquid that helps it digest insects. Other carnivorous plants found in the bog also eat insects.

The Venus' flytrap eats insects.

Bogs may not seem like very friendly homes for plants. Yet many unusual plants, including a number of types of orchids, are found there.

Bogs are very similar to fens, another type of wetland. Both form when plants die and dead plant matter piles up rather than decays. Dead plants usually rot away, but in places where temperatures are low, the ground is wet, and there is little oxygen, this decay slows down or does not happen at all. As the dead plants are tightly pressed together, they form a thick material called peat.

Bogs and fens have three basic layers. The bottom layer is the water, which makes the area a wetland. The middle layer is the peat, which grows thicker as more plants die year after year. This layer of peat can be up to 40 feet deep. Living plants are the top layer, which is where animals also live.

Bogs and fens both form peat, but they are not identical. In a bog, the peat comes from a kind of moss called sphagnum moss. Some bogs form when moss grows on land. The sphagnum moss acts like a giant sponge, soaking up the rain or snow.

Other bogs form when peat builds up over a lake or pond. Sphagnum moss grows at the edge of a lake, and over time, it slowly covers the entire lake. The water is trapped under a thick mat of peat and moss. Bogs that cover lakes completely are called "quaking bogs." They shake when people walk on the top layer.

In a fen, peat is formed by a buildup of dead grasses and sedges. These plants can grow in fens because a fen has a different water supply than a bog. Bogs rely only on precipitation for water. Fens are fed by both groundwater, or water that lies within the ground, and rain or snow. The water in a fen is moving, unlike a bog where the water is **stagnant**.

Groundwater has more nutrients than rain or snow. These nutrients create a good home for a fen's grasslike plants.

Not many creatures live in bogs and fens. Many mammals require dry nest sites, protective shelter, or burrowing areas. Bogs and fens do not provide these. Some small mammals that do live in bogs and fens are shrews and voles. Larger mammals, like moose and deer, eat the plants at the edges of bogs and fens.

a salamander in a bog

Turtles and snakes live in fens and bogs. Bogs are also home to salamanders and frogs. Fish are not found in bogs, but trout have been seen in fens.

Many insects thrive in both fens and bogs, including dragonflies and mosquitoes. The insects attract bats that come swooping out at night and birds that feed by day.

Endangered Wetlands

There is only one place in the world where alligators and crocodiles live side by side. That place is the Everglades National Park, a 1.5 million acre wetlands area in southern Florida. This park is America's biggest marsh.

The Everglades is a wide, shallow river that flows south from Lake Okeechobee to Florida Bay and the Gulf of Mexico. Fifty miles wide in some locations, the water in the Everglades might be 3 feet deep or a mere 6 inches.

The wood stork, found in the Everglades, is an endangered bird.

Many different creatures make their homes in the Everglades. Some of the wetland creatures that live in the Everglades are **endangered**, such as wood storks, Florida panthers, and American crocodiles. There are so few of these animals left that there is a danger that they will die out completely, making them **extinct** in the near future.

Humans are the reason that these wetland animals are endangered. Years ago, canals were dug in the Everglades to control the water flow and prevent the river from flooding peoples' homes and businesses. Sadly, this project badly damaged the Everglades **ecosystem**.

Some wetlands have been completely drained to make it easier for humans to survive. This has happened across the United States, including parts of the Everglades.

Farmers drained some of the wetlands so that the water could be used for their crops and for more land to raise animals. Other people drained them to build offices and homes. However, when wetlands are drained, plants and animals' homes are destroyed. When that happens, wetland creatures must find another place to live.

However, people have not always been willing to share their land with the animals of the wetlands. For example, alligators often eat small mammals that come too close to the water. What would happen if someone's dog went near the water for a cool drink or decided to jump in for a swim?

Conservation groups across the United States are working to solve the problem of threatened wetlands and wildlife. Protecting the remaining wetlands is one solution.

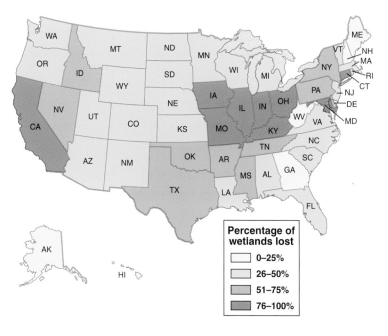

Wetlands continue to be lost today.

Restoring former wetlands to their original state and creating new wetlands are other ways to provide homes for endangered animals. The U.S. Environmental Protection Agency offers a program to help restore local wetlands. It brings together partners from students to government agencies. Groups might build a fence to keep vehicles away from a stream, or remove plants that don't belong there.

Protecting wetlands helps people as well as animals. For example, wetlands serve as a place for floodwaters to flow, keeping homes and businesses safe. Wetlands also purify the water people drink by naturally filtering water that is flowing downstream. Wetlands trap dirt and absorb substances that pollute water. In fact, when wetlands are destroyed, water treatment plants must sometimes be built to do the same job that nature can do by itself!

Everyone can take part in saving endangered wetlands. First, people should learn more about them. Then, they should support efforts to help. Finally, they should tell others how quickly wetlands are disappearing—and how important they are.

Glossary

aquatic living or growing on or near the water

carnivorous feeding only on animals

conservation the protection or restoration of natural resources

ecosystem a community of organisms and their environment

endangered in danger of dying out

epiphyte an air plant

estuary wide part of a river where it meets the sea

extinct no longer existing

floodplains lands near rivers that flood

herbivorous feeding only on plants

hydrophytes plants that can live in water or very wet soil

omnivorous feeding on both plants and animals

predators people or animals that prey upon others

stagnant not moving

tidal rising and falling due to tides